The Complete Alkaline Diet Cookbook for Beginners:

Understand pH, Eat Well with Easy Alkaline Diet Cookbook and more than 50 Delicious Recipes

2

Table of Contents

Alkaline Diet: An Introduction

Widely popular among Hollywood celebrities, the alkaline diet, also called the alkaline acid diet or the alkaline ash diet is very effective for weight loss and is believed to reduce the risk of serious conditions like cancer and arthritis. The entire diet plan is based on avoiding acidic foods. These foods include wheat, processed foods, meat, and refined sugar.

What does the diet promise?

The entire idea of the alkaline diet revolves around the fact that if you avoid acidic foods and eat more alkaline foods you are going to avoid various harmful health conditions apart from weight loss. The alkaline diet became popular when the famous fashion designer, singer, and businesswoman Victoria Beckham tweeted about it in 2013.

What to Eat & Avoid?

1. Almost all veggies and fruits, tofu and soybeans, various seeds, legumes, and nuts are allowed on this diet plan because of their alkaline nature.
2. Meat, processed foods like packaged foods, convenience foods, and canned foods, eggs, various grains, and dairy

products aren't allowed on the alkaline diet plan because of their acidic nature.

3. It's also important to note caffeine and alcohol are forbidden on this diet plan.

Tips and Benefits:

- It takes strong will power and effort to follow the alkaline diet plan because of the restrictions it carries; you'll have to say goodbye to various foods that you love. However, if you look at the benefits it offers, the restrictions are worth having a healthy lifestyle.
- The good thing about the alkaline diet plan is that all the foods on the shopping list can be easily found in a grocery store. These ingredients aren't that expensive either so the plan isn't going to be a financial burden.
- In the beginning, it'll be a bit hard to plan and prep your meals to effectively follow the diet plan. But, it isn't impossible.
- There is no exercise requirement but, if you do, you'll reap more health benefits.
- The alkaline diet is mostly based on a vegetarian diet. If you cut out dairy products, the diet is suitable for vegans too.
- The alkaline diet forbids wheat. So it is not going to be a problem for you if gluten-free is your thing.

- Apart from wheat restrictions, the alkaline diet also removes various foods known to cause food allergies from its allowed foods list. These include shellfish, peanuts, fish, milk, walnuts, and eggs. This makes the diet perfect for individuals who want to avoid sugar and fats.

Does the alkaline diet work?

Before we proceed with how effective the diet plan is, let's understand how our body works in terms of the pH scale. The pH scale is used for measuring the alkalinity or acidity of a substance. If the pH level is 0, the substance is highly acidic while a reading of 14 means the substance is highly alkaline.

The human blood is slightly alkaline and has a pH scale reading ranging between 7.35 and 7.45. The human stomach is very acidic with a pH scale reading of 3.5 or less which is effective in breaking down the food you eat. The nature of your urine is dependent on your diet plan and while the level in the blood is maintained steady by our body.

According to Dr. Melinda Ratini, a member of the WebMD medical review team, the diet is effective in many aspects. According to her, the claim by the alkaline diet that it is able to keep the pH level of your blood steady is somewhat true. But, it is important to understand that no matter what you eat your body is built to maintain the pH level of your blood on its own.

She also stated that the foods listed in the alkaline diet plan are very effective and well known for effective weight loss. Eating enough fruits and veggies, remaining hydrated and eliminating processed foods, refined sugar, and alcohol from your diet plan ensures a healthy way to lose weight.

She has also said that despite limited evidence available, a diet plan with limited to no acidic foods like bread and animal proteins (cheese and meat) and higher amount of veggies and fruits is known to reduce the risk of many diseases. These diseases include kidney stones, back pain, and type-2 diabetes. More so, this type of diet can help you maintain healthy muscles and bones in addition to boosting mental performance and cardiac health. There is still research going on to further test these claims but for now, they are considered true.

By following an alkaline diet, you're eating higher amounts of veggies and fruits while avoiding foods high in calories and fats. You'll also cut back on or eliminate prepared foods which are usually high in sodium. This is very beneficial for people with heart issues since it'll be easier to maintain steady cholesterol and blood pressure levels.

BREAKFAST RECIPES

Refreshing Red Juice

Ingredients:

- 2 beets, peeled and roughly diced
- 1 large red bell pepper, seeded and chopped
- 1 large tomato, seeded and chopped
- 2 large red apples, cored and sliced
- 2½ cups fresh strawberries, hulled and sliced
- ¼ cup fresh mint leaves

How to Prepare:

1. Add all ingredients to a juicer and extract the juice according to manufacturer's directions.

2. Transfer into two glasses and serve immediately.

Preparation time: 10 minutes
Total time: 10 minutes
Servings: 2

Nutritional Values:

- *Calories 258*
- *Total Fat 1.5 g*
- *Saturated Fat 0.1 g*
- *Cholesterol 0 mg*
- *Sodium 90 mg*
- *Total Carbs 63.6 g*
- *Fiber 13.7 g*
- *Sugar 45.4 g*
- *Protein 5.3 g*

Green Fruit Juice

Ingredients:

- 4 large kiwis, peeled and chopped
- 2 large green apples, cored and sliced
- 1 cup seedless green grapes
- 2 teaspoons lime juice

How to Prepare:

1. Add all ingredients to a juicer and extract the juice according to manufacturer's directions.
2. Transfer into two glasses and serve immediately.

Preparation time: 10 minutes

Total time: 10 minutes

Servings: 2

Nutritional Values:

- *Calories 240*
- *Total Fat 1.4 g*
- *Saturated Fat 0.1 g*
- *Cholesterol 0 mg*
- *Sodium 7 mg*
- *Total Carbs 61 g*
- *Fiber 10.4 g*
- *Sugar 44.3 g*
- *Protein 2.6 g*

Bell Pepper & Mushroom Omelet

Ingredients:

- 6 large organic eggs
- Sea salt and freshly ground black pepper, to taste
- ½ cup unsweetened almond milk
- ½ of an onion, chopped
- ¼ cup fresh mushrooms, cut into slices
- ¼ cup red bell pepper, seeded and diced
- 1 tablespoon chives, minced

How to Prepare:

1. Preheat the oven to 350 degrees F. Lightly grease a pie dish.

15

2. In a bowl, add the eggs, salt, black pepper, and almond milk and beat until well combined.

3. In another bowl, mix together the onion, bell pepper, and mushrooms.

4. Transfer the egg mixture into the prepared pie dish evenly.

5. Top with vegetable mixture evenly.

6. Sprinkle with chives evenly.

7. Bake for about 20-25 minutes.

8. With a knife, cut into equal sized wedges and serve.

Preparation time: 15 minutes

Cooking time: 25 minutes

Total time: 40 minutes

Servings: 4

Nutritional Values:

- *Calories 121*
- *Total Fat 8 g*
- *Saturated Fat 2.4 g*
- *Cholesterol 279 mg*
- *Sodium 187 mg*
- *Total Carbs 2.9 g*
- *Fiber 0.6 g*
- *Sugar 1.6 g*
- *Protein 10 g*

Tofu & Veggie Scramble

Ingredients:

- ½ tablespoon olive oil
- 1 small onion, chopped finely
- 1 small red bell pepper, seeded and chopped finely
- 1 cup cherry tomatoes, chopped finely
- 1½ cups firm tofu, crumbled and chopped
- Pinch of cayenne pepper
- Pinch of ground turmeric
- Sea salt, to taste

How to Prepare:

1. In a skillet, heat oil over medium heat and sauté the onion and bell pepper for about 4-5 minute.

2. Add the tomatoes and cook for about 1-2 minutes.
3. Add the tofu, turmeric, cayenne pepper and salt and cook for about 6-8 minutes.
4. Serve hot.

Preparation time: 15 minutes
Cooking time: 15 minutes
Total time: 30 minutes
Servings: 2

Nutritional Values:

- *Calories 212*
- *Total Fat 11.8 g*
- *Saturated Fat 2.2 g*
- *Cholesterol 0 mg*
- *Sodium 147 mg*
- *Total Carbs 14.6 g*
- *Fiber 4.4 g*
- *Sugar 8 g*
- *Protein 17.3 g*

Apple Porridge

Ingredients:

- 2 cups unsweetened almond milk
- 3 tablespoons walnuts, chopped
- 3 tablespoons sunflower seeds
- 2 large apples, peeled, cored, and grated
- ½ teaspoon organic vanilla extract
- Pinch of ground cinnamon
- ½ small apple, cored and sliced

How to Prepare:

1. In a large pan, mix together the milk, walnuts, sunflower seeds, grated apple, vanilla, and cinnamon over medium-low heat and cook for about 3-5 minutes.

2. Remove from the heat and transfer the porridge into serving bowls.
3. Top with remaining apple slices and serve.

Preparation time: 10 minutes
Cooking time: 5 minutes
Total time: 15 minutes
Servings: 4

Nutritional Values:

- *Calories 143*
- *Total Fat 6.6 g*
- *Saturated Fat 0.5 g*
- *Cholesterol 0 mg*
- *Sodium 92 mg*
- *Total Carbs 21.4 g*
- *Fiber 4.5 g*
- *Sugar 14.7 g*
- *Protein 2.7 g*

Overnight Chocolate Oatmeal

Ingredients:

- 1 cup unsweetened almond milk
- 1 cup rolled oats
- 1 tablespoon cacao powder
- 8-10 drops liquid stevia
- ¼ cup fresh blueberries
- 1 tablespoon unsweetened dark mini chocolate chips

How to Prepare:

1. In a large bowl, add all the ingredients except blueberries and chocolate chips and mix until well combined.
2. Cover the bowl and refrigerate overnight.
3. Top with chocolate chips and blueberries and serve.

21

Preparation time: 10 minutes

Total time: 10 minutes

Servings: 2

Nutritional Values:

- *Calories 209*
- *Total Fat 6 g*
- *Saturated Fat 1.5 g*
- *Cholesterol 0 mg*
- *Sodium 93 mg*
- *Total Carbs 35.1 g*
- *Fiber 5.8 g*
- *Sugar 4.2 g*
- *Protein 6.8 g*

Simple Bread

Ingredients:

- 4 cups spelt flour
- 4 tablespoons sesame seeds
- 1 teaspoon baking soda
- ¼ teaspoon sea salt
- 10-12 drops liquid stevia
- 2 cups plus 2 tablespoons unsweetened almond milk

How to Prepare:

1. Preheat oven to 350 degrees F. Line a 9x5-inch loaf pan with greased parchment paper.
2. In a large bowl, add all the ingredients and mix until well combined.

3. Transfer the mixture to the prepared loaf pan evenly.
4. Bake for 1 hour and 10 minutes or until a toothpick inserted in the center comes out clean.
5. Remove from oven and place the loaf pan onto a wire rack to cool for at least 10 minutes.
6. Carefully, invert the bread onto the rack to cool completely.
7. With a sharp knife, cut the bread loaf into desired sized slices and serve.

Preparation time: 10 minutes
Cooking time: 1 hour 10 minutes
Total time: 1 hour 20 minutes
Servings: 8 1-inch thick slices

Nutritional Values:

- *Calories 239*
- *Total Fat 4.2 g*
- *Saturated Fat 0.6 g*
- *Cholesterol 0 mg*
- *Sodium 281 mg*
- *Total Carbs 45.1 g*
- *Fiber 8.1 g*
- *Sugar 0.3 g*
- *Protein 9.3 g*

Zucchini Bread

Ingredients:

- ½ cup almond flour, sifted

- 1½ teaspoons baking soda

- ½ teaspoon ground cinnamon

- ¼ teaspoon ground cardamom

- 1½ cups banana, peeled and mashed

- ¼ cup almond butter, softened

- 2 teaspoons organic vanilla extract

- 1 cup zucchini, shredded

25

How to Prepare:

1. Preheat oven to 350 degrees F. Grease a 6x3-inch loaf pan.

2. In a large bowl, mix together the flour, baking soda, and spices.

3. In another bowl, add the remaining ingredients except zucchini and beat until well combined.

4. Add the flour mixture and mix until just combined.

5. Fold in the grated zucchini.

6. Transfer the batter into the prepared loaf pan.

7. Bake for about 40-45 minutes or until a toothpick inserted in the center comes out clean.

8. Remove from oven and place the loaf pan onto a wire rack to cool for at least 10 minutes.

9. Carefully, invert the bread onto the rack to cool completely before slicing.

10. With a sharp knife, cut the bread loaf into 6 equal sized slices and serve.

Preparation time: 15 minutes

Cooking time: 45 minutes

Total time: 1 hour

Servings: 6 1-inch thick slices

Nutritional Values:

- *Calories 161*
- *Total Fat 10.5 g*
- *Saturated Fat 1.5 g*
- *Cholesterol 0 mg*
- *Sodium 319 mg*
- *Total Carbs 14.7 g*
- *Fiber 2.6 g*
- *Sugar 5.5 g*
- *Protein 4.7 g*

Vanilla Waffles

Ingredients:

- ¼ cup coconut flour
- 1 teaspoon baking powder
- 6 organic egg whites
- ¼ cup unsweetened almond milk
- 1 tablespoon agave syrup
- 1/8 teaspoon organic vanilla extract
- 4-6 fresh strawberries, hulled and sliced

How to Prepare:

1. Preheat the waffle iron and lightly grease it.
2. In a large bowl, add the flour and baking powder and mix well.

3. Add the remaining ingredients except the strawberries and mix until well combined.
4. Place half of the mixture to the preheated waffle iron.
5. Cook for about 3-5 minutes or until waffles become golden brown.
6. Repeat with the remaining mixture.
7. Serve warm topped with the strawberry slices.

Preparation time: 10 minutes
Cooking time: 10 minutes
Total time: 20 minutes
Servings: 2

Nutritional Values:

- *Calories 107*
- *Total Fat 0.9 g*
- *Saturated Fat 0.3 g*
- *Cholesterol 0 mg*
- *Sodium 136 mg*
- *Total Carbs 13.4 g*
- *Fiber 1.3 g*
- *Sugar 2 g*
- *Protein 11.3 g*

Banana Pancakes

Ingredients:
- ¼ cup rolled oats
- ¼ cup arrowroot flour
- ½ teaspoon organic baking powder
- ¼ teaspoon organic baking soda
- 1/8 teaspoon ground cinnamon
- ¼ cup unsweetened almond milk
- 2 organic egg whites
- 2 teaspoons almond butter
- ½ banana, peeled and mashed well
- 1/8 teaspoon organic vanilla extract
- 1 teaspoon olive oil
- ½ banana, peeled and sliced

How to Prepare:

1. In a large bowl, add the flour, oats, baking soda, baking powder, and cinnamon and mix well.
2. In another bowl, add the almond milk, egg whites, almond butter, mashed banana, and vanilla and beat until well combined.
3. Add the flour mixture and mix until well combined.
4. In a large frying pan, heat the oil over medium-low heat.
5. Add half of the mixture and cook for about 1-2 minutes.
6. Flip to the other side and cook for 1-2 minutes more.
7. Repeat with the remaining mixture.
8. Serve topped with banana slices.

Preparation time: 15 minutes

Cooking time: 8 minutes

Total time: 23 minutes

Servings: 2

Nutritional Values:

- *Calories 244*
- *Total Fat 12.7 g*
- *Saturated Fat 1.3 g*
- *Cholesterol 0 mg*
- *Sodium 222 mg*
- *Total Carbs 26.6 g*
- *Fiber 4.6 g*
- *Sugar 8.3 g*
- *Protein 9.8 g*

SMOOTHIE RECIPES

Banana Smoothie

Ingredients:

- 2 cups chilled unsweetened almond milk
- 1 large frozen banana, peeled and sliced
- 1 tablespoon almonds, chopped
- 1 teaspoon organic vanilla extract

How to Prepare:

1. Place all the ingredients in a high-speed blender and pulse until creamy.
2. Pour the smoothie into two glasses and serve immediately.

Preparation time: 10 minutes

Total time: 10 minutes

Servings: 2

Nutritional Values:

- *Calories 124*
- *Total Fat 5.2 g*
- *Saturated Fat 0.5 g*
- *Cholesterol 0 mg*
- *Sodium 181 mg*
- *Total Carbs 18.4 g*
- *Fiber 3.1 g*
- *Sugar 8.7 g*
- *Protein 2.4 g*

Strawberry Smoothie

Ingredients:

- 2 cups chilled unsweetened almond milk
- 1½ cups frozen strawberries
- 1 banana, peeled and sliced
- ¼ teaspoon organic vanilla extract

How to Prepare:

1. Add all the ingredients in a high-speed blender and pulse until smooth.
2. Pour the smoothie into two glasses and serve immediately.

Preparation time: 10 minutes

Total time: 10 minutes

Servings: 2

Nutritional Values:

- *Calories 131*
- *Total Fat 3.7 g*
- *Saturated Fat 0.4 g*
- *Cholesterol 0 mg*
- *Sodium 181 mg*
- *Total Carbs 25.3 g*
- *Fiber 4.8 g*
- *Sugar 14 g*
- *Protein 1.6 g*

Raspberry & Tofu Smoothie

Ingredients:

- 1½ cups fresh raspberries
- 6 ounces firm silken tofu, drained
- 1/8 teaspoon coconut extract
- 1 teaspoon powdered stevia
- 1½ cups unsweetened almond milk
- ¼ cup ice cubes, crushed

How to Prepare:

1. Add all the ingredients in a high-speed blender and pulse until smooth.

2. Pour the smoothie into two glasses and serve immediately.

Preparation time: 15 minutes

Total time: 15 minutes

Servings: 2

Nutritional Values:

- *Calories 131*
- *Total Fat 5.5 g*
- *Saturated Fat 0.6 g*
- *Cholesterol 0 mg*
- *Sodium 167 mg*
- *Total Carbs 14.6 g*
- *Fiber 6.8 g*
- *Sugar 5.2 g*
- *Protein 7.7 g*

Mango Smoothie

Ingredients:

- 2 cups frozen mango, peeled, pitted and chopped
- ¼ cup almond butter
- Pinch of ground turmeric
- 2 tablespoons fresh lemon juice
- 1¼ cups unsweetened almond milk
- ¼ cup ice cubes

How to Prepare:

1. Add all the ingredients in a high-speed blender and pulse until smooth.

2. Pour the smoothie into two glasses and serve immediately.

Preparation time: 10 minutes

Total time: 10 minutes

Servings: 2

Nutritional Values:

- *Calories 140*
- *Total Fat 4.1 g*
- *Saturated Fat 0.6 g*
- *Cholesterol 0 mg*
- *Sodium 118 mg*
- *Total Carbs 26.8 g*
- *Fiber 3.6 g*
- *Sugar 23 g*
- *Protein 2.5 g*

Pineapple Smoothie

Ingredients:

- 2 cups pineapple, chopped
- ½ teaspoon fresh ginger, peeled and chopped
- ½ teaspoon ground turmeric
- 1 teaspoon natural immune support supplement *
- 1 teaspoon chia seeds
- 1½ cups cold green tea
- ½ cup ice, crushed

How to Prepare:

1. Add all the ingredients in a high-speed blender and pulse until smooth.

2. Pour the smoothie into two glasses and serve immediately.

Preparation time: 10 minutes
Total time: 10 minutes
Servings: 2

Nutritional Values:

- *Calories 152*
- *Total Fat 1 g*
- *Saturated Fat 0 g*
- *Cholesterol 0 mg*
- *Sodium 9 mg*
- *Total Carbs 30 g*
- *Fiber 3.5 g*
- *Sugar 29.8 g*
- *Protein 1.5 g*

*note: this supplement is packed with about 20-25 proteins, vitamins, herbs and superfoods that boost the immune system of the body.

Kale & Pineapple Smoothie

Ingredients:

- 1½ cups fresh kale, trimmed and chopped

- 1 frozen banana, peeled and chopped

- ½ cup fresh pineapple chunks

- 1 cup unsweetened coconut milk

- ½ cup fresh orange juice

- ½ cup ice

How to Prepare:

1. Add all the ingredients in a high-speed blender and pulse until smooth.

2. Pour the smoothie into two glasses and serve immediately.

Preparation time: 15 minutes

Total time: 15 minutes

Servings: 2

Nutritional Values:

- *Calories 148*
- *Total Fat 2.4 g*
- *Saturated Fat 2.1 g*
- *Cholesterol 0 mg*
- *Sodium 23 mg*
- *Total Carbs 31.6 g*
- *Fiber 3.5 g*
- *Sugar 16.5 g*
- *Protein 2.8 g*

Green Veggies Smoothie

Ingredients:
- 1 medium avocado, peeled, pitted, and chopped
- 1 large cucumber, peeled and chopped
- 2 fresh tomatoes, chopped
- 1 small green bell pepper, seeded and chopped
- 1 cup fresh spinach, torn
- 2 tablespoons fresh lime juice
- 2 tablespoons homemade vegetable broth
- 1 cup alkaline water

How to Prepare:
1. Add all the ingredients in a high-speed blender and pulse until smooth.

2. Pour the smoothie into glasses and serve immediately.

Preparation time: 15 minutes
Total time: 15 minutes
Servings: 2

Nutritional Values:

- *Calories 275*
- *Total Fat 20.3 g*
- *Saturated Fat 4.2 g*
- *Cholesterol 0 mg*
- *Sodium 76 mg*
- *Total Carbs 24.1 g*
- *Fiber 10.1 g*
- *Sugar 9.3 g*
- *Protein 5.3 g*

Avocado & Spinach Smoothie

Ingredients:

- 2 cups fresh baby spinach
- ½ avocado, peeled, pitted, and chopped
- 4-6 drops liquid stevia
- ½ teaspoon ground cinnamon
- 1 tablespoon hemp seeds
- 2 cups chilled alkaline water

How to Prepare:

1. Add all the ingredients in a high-speed blender and pulse until smooth.

2. Pour the smoothie into two glasses and serve
    immediately.

Preparation time: 10 minutes

Total time: 10 minutes

Servings: 2

Nutritional Values:

- *Calories 132*
- *Total Fat 11.7 g*
- *Saturated Fat 2.2 g*
- *Cholesterol 0 mg*
- *Sodium 27 mg*
- *Total Carbs 6.1 g*
- *Fiber 4.5 g*
- *Sugar 0.4 g*
- *Protein 3.1 g*

Cucumber Smoothie

Ingredients:

- 1 small cucumber, peeled and chopped
- 2 cups mixed fresh greens (spinach, kale, beet greens), trimmed and chopped
- ½ cup lettuce, torn
- ¼ cup fresh parsley leaves
- ¼ cup fresh mint leaves
- 2-3 drops liquid stevia
- 1 teaspoon fresh lemon juice
- 1½ cups filtered water
- ¼ cup ice cubes

How to Prepare:

- *Add all the ingredients in a high-speed blender and pulse until smooth.*
- *Pour the smoothie into two glasses and serve immediately.*

Preparation time: 15 minutes

Total time: 15 minutes

Servings: 2

Nutritional Values:

- *Calories 50*
- *Total Fat 0.5 g*
- *Saturated Fat 0.2 g*
- *Cholesterol 0 mg*
- *Sodium 34 mg*
- *Total Carbs 11.3 g*
- *Fiber 3.6 g*
- *Sugar 3.2 g*
- *Protein 2.5 g*

LUNCH RECIPES

Mango & Avocado Salad

Ingredients:

- 2½ cups mango, peeled, pitted, and sliced
- 2½ cups avocado, peeled, pitted, and sliced
- 1 red onion, sliced
- 6 cups fresh baby arugula
- ¼ cup fresh mint leaves, chopped
- 2 tablespoons fresh orange juice
- Sea salt, to taste

How to Prepare:

1. Place all the ingredients in a large serving bowl and gently toss to combine.

2. Cover and refrigerate to chill before serving.

Preparation time: 15 minutes

Total time: 15 minutes

Servings: 6

Nutritional Values:

- *Calories 182*
- *Total Fat 12.3 g*
- *Saturated Fat 2.9 g*
- *Cholesterol 0 mg*
- *Sodium 51 mg*
- *Total Carbs 18.8 g*
- *Fiber 6.2 g*
- *Sugar 11.3 g*
- *Protein 2.6 g*

Cucumber & Tomato Salad

Ingredients:

- 2 cups plum tomatoes, chopped
- 2 cups cucumbers, chopped
- 2 cups mixed fresh lettuce, torn
- 2 cups fresh baby spinach
- 2 tablespoons extra virgin olive oil
- 2 tablespoons fresh lime juice
- Sea salt, to taste

How to Prepare:

1. Place all the ingredients in a large serving bowl and gently toss to combine.

2. Serve immediately.

Preparation time: 15 minutes
Total time: 15 minutes
Servings: 4

Nutritional Values:

- *Calories 96*
- *Total Fat 7.4 g*
- *Saturated Fat 1.1 g*
- *Cholesterol 0 mg*
- *Sodium 85 mg*
- *Total Carbs 7.9 g*
- *Fiber 1.8 g*
- *Sugar 4.8 g*
- *Protein 2 g*

Broccoli Soup

Ingredients:

- 2 tablespoons olive oil
- ½ cup onion, chopped
- 1 garlic clove, minced
- 1 tablespoon fresh thyme, chopped
- ¼ teaspoon ground cumin
- ¼ teaspoon red pepper flakes, crushed
- 2 medium heads broccoli, cut into florets
- 4 cups homemade vegetable broth
- 1 avocado, peeled, pitted, and chopped

How to Prepare:

1. In a large soup pan, heat the oil over medium heat and sauté the onion for about 4-5 minutes.

2. Add the garlic, thyme, and spices and sauté for about 1 minute more.
3. Add the broccoli and cook for about 3-4 minutes.
4. Stir in the broth and bring to a boil over high heat.
5. Reduce the heat to medium-low.
6. Cover the soup pan and cook for 32-35 minutes.
7. Remove from the heat and set aside to cool slightly.
8. In a blender, place the mixture in batches with avocado and pulse until smooth.
9. Serve immediately.

Preparation time: 15 minutes
Cooking time: 45 minutes
Total time: 1 hour
Servings: 4

Nutritional Values:
- *Calories 254*
- *Total Fat 18.7 g*
- *Saturated Fat 3.5 g*
- *Cholesterol 0 mg*
- *Sodium 810 mg*
- *Total Carbs 15.8 g*
- *Fiber 7.3 g*
- *Sugar 3.8 g*
- *Protein 9.7 g*

Pumpkin Soup

Ingredients:

- 2 teaspoons olive oil
- 1 onion, chopped
- 1 teaspoon fresh ginger, chopped
- 2 garlic cloves, chopped
- 2 tablespoons fresh cilantro, chopped
- 3 cups pumpkin, peeled and cubed
- 4¼ cups homemade vegetable broth
- Sea salt and freshly ground black pepper, to taste
- ½ cup coconut cream
- 2 tablespoons fresh lime juice

How to Prepare:

1. In a large soup pan, heat oil over medium heat and sauté the onion, ginger, garlic, and cilantro for about 3-4 minutes.
2. Add the pumpkin and broth and bring to a boil.
3. Turn the heat to low and simmer covered for about 15 minutes.
4. Remove from heat and set aside to cool slightly.
5. Transfer the mixture into a high-speed blender in batches with coconut cream and pulse until smooth.
6. Return the soup into the pan over medium heat and cook for 3 minutes or until hot enough.
7. Stir in the lime juice and serve hot.

Preparation time: 15 minutes

Cooking time: 25 minutes

Total time: 40 minutes

Servings: 4

Nutritional Values:

- *Calories 208*
- *Total Fat 11.5 g*
- *Saturated Fat 7.4 g*
- *Cholesterol 0 mg*
- *Sodium 885 mg*
- *Total Carbs 21 g*
- *Fiber 6.7 g*
- *Sugar 9 g*
- *Protein 8.3 g*

Nutty Brussels Sprouts

Ingredients:

- ½ pound Brussels sprouts, halved
- 1 tablespoon olive oil
- 2 garlic cloves, minced
- ½ teaspoon red pepper flakes, crushed
- Sea salt and freshly ground black pepper, to taste
- 1 tablespoon fresh lemon juice
- 1 tablespoon pine nuts

How to Prepare:

1. Arrange a steamer basket in a large pan of boiling water.
2. Place the Brussels sprouts in steamer basket and steam, covered for about 6-8 minutes.

3. Drain the Brussels sprouts well.

4. In a large skillet, heat the oil over medium heat and sauté the garlic and red pepper flakes for about 40 seconds.

5. Stir in the Brussels sprouts, salt, and black pepper and sauté for about 4-5 minutes.

6. Stir in lemon juice and sauté for about 1 minute more.

7. Stir in the pine nuts and remove from the heat.

8. Serve hot.

Preparation time: 15 minutes

Cooking time: 15 minutes

Total time: 30 minutes

Servings: 2

Nutritional Values:

- *Calories 146*
- *Total Fat 10.5 g*
- *Saturated Fat 1.4 g*
- *Cholesterol 0 mg*
- *Sodium 148 mg*
- *Total Carbs 12.3 g*
- *Fiber 4.6 g*
- *Sugar 2.8 g*
- *Protein 4.8 g*

Roasted Butternut Squash

Ingredients:

- 8 cups butternut squash, peeled, seeded, and cubed
- 2 tablespoons melted almond butter
- ½ teaspoon ground cinnamon
- ½ teaspoon ground cumin
- ¼ teaspoon red pepper flakes
- Sea salt, to taste

How to Prepare:

1. Preheat oven to 425 degrees F. Arrange pieces of foil on 2 baking sheets.

2. In a large bowl, add all the ingredients and toss to coat well.
3. Arrange the squash pieces onto the prepared baking sheets in a single layer.
4. Roast for about 40-45 minutes.
5. Remove from the oven and serve.

Preparation time: 15 minutes
Cooking time: 45 minutes
Total time: 1 hour
Servings: 6

Nutritional Values:

- *Calories 118*
- *Total Fat 3.2 g*
- *Saturated Fat 0.3 g*
- *Cholesterol 0 mg*
- *Sodium 47 mg*
- *Total Carbs 23.1 g*
- *Fiber 4.4 g*
- *Sugar 4.4 g*
- *Protein 3.1 g*

Broccoli with Bell Pepper

Ingredients:

- 2 tablespoons olive oil
- 4 garlic cloves, minced
- 1 large white onion, sliced
- 2 cups small broccoli florets
- 3 red bell peppers, seeded and sliced
- ¼ cup homemade vegetable broth
- Sea salt and freshly ground black pepper, to taste

How to Prepare:

1. In a large skillet, heat the oil over medium heat and sauté the garlic for about 1 minute.
2. Add the onion, broccoli, and bell peppers and stir fry for

about 5 minutes.

3. Add the broth and stir fry for about 4 minutes more.

4. Serve hot.

Preparation time: 15 minutes

Cooking time: 10 minutes

Total time: 25 minutes

Servings: 4

Nutritional Values:

- *Calories 126*
- *Total Fat 7.5 g*
- *Saturated Fat 1 g*
- *Cholesterol 0 mg*
- *Sodium 125 mg*
- *Total Carbs 14.3 g*
- *Fiber 2.3 g*
- *Sugar 6.9 g*
- *Protein 3.1 g*

Tamari Shrimp

Ingredients:

- 1 tablespoon olive oil
- 2 garlic cloves, minced
- ½ pound raw jumbo shrimp, peeled and deveined
- 2 tablespoons tamari
- Freshly ground black pepper, to taste

How to Prepare:

1. In a large skillet, heat the oil over medium heat and sauté the garlic for about 1 minute.
2. Stir in the shrimp, tamari and black pepper and cook for about 4-5 minutes or until done completely.

3. Serve hot.

Preparation time: 15 minutes

Cooking time: 6 minutes

Total time: 21 minutes

Servings: 2

Nutritional Values:

- *Calories 156*
- *Total Fat 7 g*
- *Saturated Fat 1 g*
- *Cholesterol 233 mg*
- *Sodium 2000 mg*
- *Total Carbs 2 g*
- *Fiber 0.2 g*
- *Sugar 2.4 g*
- *Protein 22.3 g*

Veggie Kebabs

Ingredients:

For Marinade:

- 2 garlic cloves, minced
- 2 teaspoons fresh basil, minced
- 2 teaspoons fresh oregano, minced
- ½ teaspoon cayenne pepper
- Sea salt and freshly ground black pepper, to taste
- 2 tablespoons fresh lemon juice
- 2 tablespoons olive oil

For Veggies:

- 2 large zucchinis, cut into thick slices
- 8 large button mushrooms, quartered
- 1 yellow bell pepper, seeded and cubed
- 1 red bell pepper, seeded and cubed

How to Prepare:

1. For marinade: in a large bowl, add all the ingredients and mix until well combined.
2. Add the vegetables to the marinade and toss to coat well.
3. Cover and refrigerate to marinate the veggies for at least 6-8 hours.
4. In a large bowl of the water, soak the wooden skewers for at least 30 minutes.
5. Preheat the grill to medium-high heat. Generously grease the grill grate.
6. Remove the vegetables from the bowl and discard the marinade.
7. Thread the vegetables onto the pre-soaked wooden skewers, starting with the zucchini, mushrooms and bell peppers.
8. Grill for about 8-10 minutes or until done completely, flipping occasionally.

Preparation time: 20 minutes

Cooking time: 10 minutes

Total time: 30 minutes

Servings: 4

Nutritional Values:

- *Calories 122*
- *Total Fat 7.8 g*
- *Saturated Fat 1.2 g*
- *Cholesterol 0 mg*
- *Sodium 81 mg*
- *Total Carbs 12.7 g*
- *Fiber 3.5 g*
- *Sugar 6.8g*
- *Protein 4.3 g*

DINNER RECIPES

Quinoa & Chickpea Salad

Ingredients:

- 1¾ cups homemade vegetable broth
- 1 cup quinoa, rinsed
- Sea salt, to taste
- 1½ cups cooked chickpeas
- 1 medium green bell pepper, seeded and chopped
- 1 medium red bell pepper, seeded and chopped
- 2 cucumbers, chopped
- ½ cup scallion (green part only), chopped
- 1 tablespoon olive oil
- 2 tablespoons fresh cilantro leaves, chopped

69

How to Prepare:

1. In a pan, add the broth and bring to a boil over high heat.
2. Add the quinoa and salt and cook until boiling again.
3. Reduce the heat to low and simmer covered for about 15-20 minutes or until all the liquid is absorbed.
4. Remove from the heat and set aside still covered for about 5-10 minutes.
5. Uncover and fluff the quinoa with a fork.
6. In a large serving bowl, add the quinoa and the remaining ingredients and gently toss to coat.
7. Serve immediately.

Preparation time: 20 minutes
Cooking time: 20 minutes
Total time: 40 minutes
Servings: 6

Nutritional Values:

- *Calories 348*
- *Total Fat 7.7 g*
- *Saturated Fat 1 g*
- *Cholesterol 0 mg*
- *Sodium 280 mg*
- *Total Carbs 56 g*
- *Fiber 11.9 g*
- *Sugar 9.4 g*
- *Protein 16.3 g*

Mixed Veggie Soup

Ingredients:

- 1½ tablespoons olive oil
- 4 medium carrots, peeled and chopped
- 1 medium onion, chopped
- 2 garlic cloves, minced
- 2 celery stalks, chopped
- 2 cups fresh tomatoes, chopped finely
- 3 cups small cauliflower florets
- 3 cups small broccoli florets
- 3 cups frozen peas
- 8 cups homemade vegetable broth
- 3 tablespoons fresh lemon juice
- Sea salt, to taste

How to Prepare:

1. In a large soup pan, heat the oil over medium heat and sauté the carrots, celery, and onion for 6 minutes.
2. Stir in the garlic and sauté for about 1 minute.
3. Add the tomatoes and cook for about 2-3 minutes, crushing them with the back of a spoon.
4. Add the vegetables and broth and bring to a boil over high heat.
5. Reduce the heat to low.
6. Cover the pan and simmer for about 30-35 minutes.
7. Mix in the lemon juice and salt and remove from the heat.
8. Serve hot.

Preparation time: 15 minutes
Cooking time: 45 minutes
Total time: 1 hour
Servings: 8

Nutritional Values:

- *Calories 1587*
- *Total Fat 4.5 g*
- *Saturated Fat 0.9 g*
- *Cholesterol 0 mg*
- *Sodium 888 mg*
- *Total Carbs 20.1 g*
- *Fiber 6.9 g*
- *Sugar 8.4 g*
- *Protein 10.5 g*

Beans & Barley Soup

Ingredients:

- 1 tablespoon olive oil
- 1 white onion, chopped
- 2 celery stalks, chopped
- 1 large carrot, peeled and chopped
- 2 tablespoons fresh rosemary, chopped
- 2 garlic cloves, minced
- 4 cups fresh tomatoes, chopped
- 4 cups homemade vegetable broth
- 1 cup pearl barley
- 2 cups cooked white beans
- 2 tablespoons fresh lemon juice
- 4 tablespoons fresh parsley leaves, chopped

How to Prepare:

1. In a large soup pan, heat the oil over medium heat and sauté the onion, celery, and carrot for about 4-5 minutes.
2. Add the garlic and rosemary and sauté for about 1 minute.
3. Add the tomatoes and cook for 3-4 minutes, crushing them with the back of a spoon.
4. Add the barley and broth and bring to a boil.
5. Reduce the heat to low and simmer covered for about 20-25 minutes.
6. Stir in the beans and lemon juice and simmer for about 5 minutes more.
7. Garnish with parsley and serve hot

Preparation time: 15 minutes
Cooking time: 40 minutes
Total time: 55 minutes
Servings: 4

Nutritional Values:

- *Calories 407*
- *Total Fat 7.2 g*
- *Saturated Fat 1.2 g*
- *Cholesterol 0 mg*
- *Sodium 841 mg*
- *Total Carbs 70.3 g*
- *Fiber 16.9 g*
- *Sugar 8.2 g*
- *Protein 18.3 g*

Tofu & Bell Pepper Stew

Ingredients:

- 2 tablespoons garlic
- 1 jalapeño pepper, seeded and chopped
- 1 (16-ounce) jar roasted red peppers, rinsed, drained, and chopped
- 2 cups homemade vegetable broth
- 2 cups filtered water
- 1 medium green bell pepper, seeded and sliced thinly
- 1 medium red bell pepper, seeded and sliced thinly
- 1 (16-ounce) package extra-firm tofu, drained and cubed
- 1 (10-ounce) package frozen baby spinach, thawed

How to Prepare:

1. Add the garlic, jalapeño pepper, and roasted red peppers in a food processor and pulse until smooth.
2. In a large pan, add the puree, broth, and water and cook until boiling over medium-high heat.
3. Add the bell peppers and tofu and stir to combine.
4. Reduce the heat to medium and cook for about 5 minutes.
5. Stir in the spinach and cook for about 5 minutes.
6. Serve hot.

Preparation time: 15 minutes
Cooking time: 15 minutes
Total time: 30 minutes
Servings: 6

Nutritional Values:

- *Calories 130*
- *Total Fat 5.3 g*
- *Saturated Fat 0.6 g*
- *Cholesterol 0 mg*
- *Sodium 482 mg*
- *Total Carbs 12.2 g*
- *Fiber 2.9 g*
- *Sugar 6.2 g*
- *Protein 11.8 g*

Chickpea Stew

Ingredients:

- 1 tablespoon olive oil
- 1 medium onion, chopped
- 2 cups carrots, peeled and chopped
- 2 garlic cloves, minced
- 1 teaspoon red pepper flakes
- 2 large tomatoes, peeled, seeded, and chopped finely
- 2 cups homemade vegetable broth
- 2 cups cooked chickpeas
- 2 cups fresh spinach, chopped
- 1 tablespoon fresh lemon juice
- Sea salt and freshly ground black pepper, to taste

How to Prepare:

1. In a large pan, heat oil over medium heat and sauté the onion and carrot for about 6 minutes.
2. Stir in the garlic and red pepper flakes and sauté for about 1 minute.
3. Add the tomatoes and cook for about 2-3 minutes.
4. Add the broth and bring to a boil.
5. Reduce the heat to low and simmer for about 10 minutes.
6. Stir in the chickpeas and simmer for about 5 minutes.
7. Stir in the spinach and simmer for 3-4 minutes more.
8. Stir in the lemon juice and seasoning and remove from the heat.
9. Serve hot.

Preparation time: 15 minutes
Cooking time: 30 minutes
Total time: 45 minutes
Servings: 4

Nutritional Values:

- *Calories 217*
- *Total Fat 6.6 g*
- *Saturated Fat 0.8 g*
- *Cholesterol 0 mg*
- *Sodium 827 mg*
- *Total Carbs 31.4 g*
- *Fiber 9.5 g*
- *Sugar 7.8 g*
- *Protein 10.6 g*

Lentils with Kale

Ingredients:
- 1½ cups red lentils
- 1½ cups homemade vegetable broth
- 1½ tablespoons olive oil
- ½ cup onion, chopped
- 1 teaspoon fresh ginger, peeled and minced
- 2 garlic cloves, minced
- 1½ cups tomato, chopped
- 6 cups fresh kale, tough ends removed and chopped
- Sea salt and ground black pepper, to taste

How to Prepare:
1. In a pan, add the broth and lentils and bring to a boil over medium-high heat.

2. Reduce the heat to low and simmer covered for about 20 minutes or until almost all the liquid is absorbed.
3. Remove from the heat and set aside still covered.
4. Meanwhile, in a large skillet, heat oil over medium heat and sauté the onion for about 5-6 minutes.
5. Add the ginger and garlic and sauté for about 1 minute.
6. Add tomatoes and kale and cook for about 4-5 minutes.
7. Stir in the lentils, salt, and black pepper then remove from heat.
8. Serve hot.

Preparation time: 15 minutes
Cooking time: 20 minutes
Total time: 35 minutes
Servings: 6

Nutritional Values:
- *Calories 257*
- *Total Fat 4.5 g*
- *Saturated Fat 0.7 g*
- *Cholesterol 0 mg*
- *Sodium 265 mg*
- *Total Carbs 39.3 g*
- *Fiber 16.5 g*
- *Sugar 2.8 g*
- *Protein 16.2 g*

Veggie Ratatouille

Ingredients:

- 6 ounces homemade tomato paste
- 3 tablespoons olive oil, divided
- ½ of an onion, chopped
- 3 tablespoons garlic, minced
- Sea salt and freshly ground black pepper, to taste
- ¾ cup filtered water
- 1 zucchini, sliced into thin circles
- 1 yellow squash, sliced into thin circles
- 1 eggplant, sliced into thin circles
- 1 red bell pepper, seeded and sliced into thin circles
- 1 yellow bell pepper, seeded and sliced into thin circles

- 1 tablespoon fresh thyme leaves, minced
- 1 tablespoon fresh lemon juice

How to Prepare:

1. Preheat oven to 375 degrees F.
2. In a bowl, add the tomato paste, 1 tablespoon of oil, onion, garlic, salt, and black pepper and mix nicely.
3. In the bottom of a 10x10-inch baking dish, spread the tomato paste mixture evenly.
4. Arrange alternating vegetable slices starting at the outer edge of the baking dish and working concentrically towards the center.
5. Drizzle the remaining oil and lemon juice over the vegetables and sprinkle them with salt and black pepper followed by the thyme.
6. Arrange a piece of parchment paper over the vegetables.
7. Bake for about 45 minutes.
8. Serve hot.

Preparation time: 20 minutes

Cooking time: 45 minutes

Total time: 1 hour 5 minutes

Servings: 4

Nutritional Values:

- *Calories 206*
- *Total Fat 11.4 g*
- *Saturated Fat 1.6 g*
- *Cholesterol 0 mg*
- *Sodium 118 mg*
- *Total Carbs 54 g*
- *Fiber 26.4 g*
- *Sugar 14.1 g*
- *Protein 5.4 g*

Baked Beans

Ingredients:

- ¼ pound dry lima beans, soaked overnight and drained
- ¼ pound dry red kidney beans, soaked overnight and drained
- 1¼ tablespoons olive oil
- 1 small yellow onion, chopped
- 4 garlic cloves, minced
- 1 teaspoon dried thyme, crushed
- ½ teaspoon ground cumin
- ½ teaspoon red pepper flakes, crushed
- ¼ teaspoon smoked paprika

- 1 tablespoon fresh lemon juice
- 1 cup homemade tomato sauce
- 1 cup homemade vegetable broth
- Sea salt and freshly ground black pepper, to taste

How to Prepare:

1. Add the beans to a large pan of boiling water and bring back to a boil.
2. Reduce the heat to low.
3. Cover the pan and cook for about 1 hour.
4. Drain the beans well.
5. Preheat the oven to 325 degrees F.
6. In a large oven-proof pan, heat the oil over medium heat and sauté the onion for about 4 minutes.
7. Add the garlic, thyme, and spices and sauté for about 1 minute.
8. Stir in the cooked beans and remaining ingredients and immediately remove from the heat.
9. Cover the pan and bake in oven for about 1 hour.
10. Serve hot.

Preparation time: 15 minutes

Cooking time: 2 hours 5 minutes

Total time: 2 hours 20 minutes

Servings: 4

Nutritional Values:

- *Calories 270*
- *Total Fat 13 g*
- *Saturated Fat 1.9 g*
- *Cholesterol 0 mg*
- *Sodium 433 mg*
- *Total Carbs 29.5 g*
- *Fiber 7.4 g*
- *Sugar 4.1 g*
- *Protein 10.6 g*

Barley Pilaf

Ingredients:

- ½ cup pearl barley

- 1 cup vegetable broth

- 2 tablespoons vegetable oil, divided

- 2 garlic cloves, minced

- ½ cup white onion, chopped

- ½ cup green olives, sliced

- ½ cup green bell pepper, seeded and chopped

- ½ cup red bell pepper, seeded and chopped

- 2 tablespoons fresh cilantro, chopped

- 2 tablespoons fresh mint leaves, chopped
- 1 tablespoon tamari

How to Prepare:

1. In a pan, add the barley and broth over medium-high heat and cook until boiling.

2. Immediately, reduce the heat to low and simmer covered for about 45 minutes or until all the liquid is evaporated.

3. In a large skillet, heat 1 tablespoon of the oil over medium-high heat and sauté the garlic for about 30 seconds.

4. Stir in the cooked barley and cook for about 3 minutes.

5. Remove from the heat and set aside.

6. In another skillet, heat the remaining oil over medium heat and sauté the onion for about 7 minutes.

7. Add the olives and bell peppers and stir fry for about 3 minutes.

8. Stir in remaining ingredients and cook for about 3 minutes.

9. Stir in the barley mixture and cook for about 3 minutes.

10. Serve hot.

Preparation time: 20 minutes

Cooking time: 1 hour 5 minutes

Total time: 1 hour 25 minutes

Servings: 4

Nutritional Values:

- *Calories 204*
- *Total Fat 10.1 g*
- *Saturated Fat 1.5 g*
- *Cholesterol 0 mg*
- *Sodium 572 mg*
- *Total Carbs 25.3 g*
- *Fiber 4.9 g*
- *Sugar 2.6 g*
- *Protein 4.8 g*

SNACK RECIPES

Bean Burgers

Ingredients:

- ½ cup walnuts
- 1 carrot, peeled and chopped
- 1 celery stalk, chopped
- 4 scallions, chopped
- 5 garlic cloves, chopped
- 2¼ cups canned black beans, rinsed and drained
- 2½ cups sweet potato, peeled and grated
- ½ teaspoon red pepper flakes, crushed
- ¼ teaspoon cayenne pepper
- Sea salt and freshly ground black pepper, to taste

How to Prepare:

1. Preheat the oven to 400 degrees F. Line a baking sheet with parchment paper.
2. In a food processor, add the walnuts and pulse until finely ground.
3. Add the carrot, celery, scallion, and garlic and pulse until chopped finely.
4. Transfer the vegetable mixture into a large bowl.
5. In the same food processor, add the beans and pulse until chopped.
6. Add 1½ cups of the sweet potato and pulse until a chunky mixture forms.
7. Transfer the bean mixture into the bowl with the vegetable mixture.
8. Stir in remaining sweet potato and spices and mix until well combined.
9. Make 8 equal sized patties from the mixture.
10. Arrange the patties onto the prepared baking sheet in a single layer.
11. Bake for about 25 minutes.
12. Serve hot.

Preparation time: 20 minutes
Cooking time: 25 minutes

Total time: 45 minutes

Servings: 8

Nutritional Values:

- *Calories 300*
- *Total Fat 5.5 g*
- *Saturated Fat 0.5 g*
- *Cholesterol 0 mg*
- *Sodium 65 mg*
- *Total Carbs 49.8 g*
- *Fiber 11.4g*
- *Sugar 5.9 g*
- *Protein 15.3 g*

Grilled Watermelon

Ingredients:

- 1 watermelon, peeled and cut into 1-inch thick wedges
- 1 garlic clove, minced finely
- 2 tablespoons fresh lime juice
- Pinch of cayenne pepper
- Pinch of sea salt

How to Prepare:

1. Preheat the grill to high heat. Grease the grill grate.
2. Grill the watermelon pieces for about 2 minutes on both sides.

3. Meanwhile, in a small bowl mix together the remaining ingredients.
4. Drizzle the watermelon slices with the lemon mixture and serve.

Preparation time: 10 minutes

Cooking time: 4 minutes

Total time: 14 minutes

Servings: 4

Nutritional Values:

- *Calories 11*
- *Total Fat 0.1 g*
- *Saturated Fat 0 g*
- *Cholesterol 0 mg*
- *Sodium 59 mg*
- *Total Carbs 2.6 g*
- *Fiber 0.2 g*
- *Sugar 1.9 g*
- *Protein 0.2 g*

Mango Salsa

Ingredients:

- 1 avocado, peeled, pitted, and cut into cubes
- 2 tablespoons fresh lime juice
- 1 mango, peeled, pitted, and cubed
- 1 cup cherry tomatoes, halved
- 1 jalapeño pepper, seeded and chopped
- 1 tablespoon fresh cilantro, chopped
- Sea salt, to taste

How to Prepare:

1. In a large bowl, add the avocado and lime juice and mix well.

.. Add the remaining ingredients and stir to combine.

3. Serve immediately.

Preparation time: 15 minutes

Total time: 15 minutes

Servings: 6

Nutritional Values:

- *Calories 108*
- *Total Fat 6.8 g*
- *Saturated Fat 1.4 g*
- *Cholesterol 0 mg*
- *Sodium 43 mg*
- *Total Carbs 12.6 g*
- *Fiber 3.6 g*
- *Sugar 8.7 g*
- *Protein 1.4 g*

Avocado Gazpacho

Ingredients:

- 3 large avocados, peeled, pitted, and chopped
- 1/3 cup fresh cilantro leaves
- 3 cups homemade vegetable broth
- 2 tablespoons fresh lemon juice
- 1 teaspoon ground cumin
- ¼ teaspoon cayenne pepper
- Sea salt, to taste

How to Prepare:

1. Add all the ingredients in a high-speed blender and pulse until smooth.

2. Transfer the soup into a large bowl.

3. Cover the bowl and refrigerate to chill for at least 2-3 hours before serving.

Preparation time: 15 minutes
Total time: 15 minutes
Servings: 6

Nutritional Values:

- *Calories 227*
- *Total Fat 20.4 g*
- *Saturated Fat 4.4 g*
- *Cholesterol 0 mg*
- *Sodium 429 mg*
- *Total Carbs 9.4 g*
- *Fiber 6.8 g*
- *Sugar 1 g*
- *Protein 4.5 g*

Roasted Chickpeas

Ingredients:

- 4 cups cooked chickpeas
- 2 garlic cloves, minced
- ½ teaspoon dried oregano, crushed
- ½ teaspoon smoked paprika
- ¼ teaspoon ground cumin
- Sea salt, to taste
- 1 tablespoon olive oil

How to Prepare:

1. Preheat the oven to 400 degrees F. Grease a large baking sheet.
2. Place chickpeas onto the prepared baking sheet in a single layer.

3. Roast for about 30 minutes, stirring the chickpeas every 10 minutes.
4. Meanwhile, in a small mixing bowl, mix together garlic, thyme, and spices.
5. Remove the baking sheet from the oven.
6. Pour the garlic mixture and oil over the chickpeas and toss to coat well.
7. Roast for about 10-15 minutes more.
8. Now, turn the oven off but leave the baking sheet inside for about 10 minutes before serving.

Preparation time: 10 minutes
Cooking time: 45 minutes
Total time: 55 minutes
Servings: 12

Nutritional Values:
- *Calories 92*
- *Total Fat 1.9 g*
- *Saturated Fat 0.2 g*
- *Cholesterol 0 mg*
- *Sodium 166 mg*
- *Total Carbs 15 g*
- *Fiber 0.1 g*
- *Sugar 4 g*
- *Protein 4.1 g*

Banana Chips

Ingredients:

- 2 large bananas, peeled and cut into ¼-inch thick slices

How to Prepare:

1. Prepare the oven to 250 degrees F. Line a large baking sheet with baking paper.
2. Place the banana slices onto the prepared baking sheet in a single layer.
3. Bake for about 1 hour.

Preparation time: 10 minutes

Cooking time: 1 hour

Total time: 1 hour 10 minutes

Servings: 4

Nutritional Values:

- *Calories 61*
- *Total Fat 0.2 g*
- *Saturated Fat 0.1 g*
- *Cholesterol 0 mg*
- *Sodium 1 mg*
- *Total Carbs 15.5 g*
- *Fiber 1.8 g*
- *Sugar 8.3 g*
- *Protein 0.7 g*

Roasted Cashews

Ingredients:

- 2 cups raw cashews
- ½ teaspoon ground cumin
- ¼ teaspoon cayenne pepper
- Pinch of salt
- 1 tablespoon fresh lemon juice

How to Prepare:

1. Preheat the oven to 400 degrees F. Line a large roasting pan with a piece of foil.
2. In a large bowl, add the cashews and spices and toss to coat well.

3. Transfer the cashews to the prepared roasting pan.

4. Roast for about 8-10 minutes.

5. Drizzle with lemon juice and serve.

Preparation time: 10 minutes

Cooking time: 10 minutes

Total time: 20 minutes

Servings: 12

Nutritional Values:

- *Calories 132*
- *Total Fat 10.6 g*
- *Saturated Fat 2.1 g*
- *Cholesterol 0 mg*
- *Sodium 16 mg*
- *Total Carbs 7.6 g*
- *Fiber 0.7 g*
- *Sugar 1.2 g*
- *Protein 3.5 g*

Dried Orange Slices

Ingredients:

* 4 seedless navel oranges, cut into thin slices (do NOT peel oranges)

How to Prepare:

1. Set the dehydrator to 135 degrees F.
2. Arrange the orange slices onto the dehydrator sheets.
3. Dehydrate for about 10 hours.

Preparation time: 10 minutes

Cooking time: 10 hours

Total time: 10 hours 10 minutes

Servings: 15

Nutritional Values:

- *Calories 23*
- *Total Fat 0.1 g*
- *Saturated Fat 0 g*
- *Cholesterol 0 mg*
- *Sodium 0 mg*
- *Total Carbs 5.8 g*
- *Fiber 3.5 g*
- *Sugar 4.6 g*
- *Protein 0.5 g*

Chickpea Hummus

Ingredients:

- 2 (15-ounce) cans chickpeas, rinsed and drained
- ½ cup tahini
- 1 garlic clove, chopped
- 2 tablespoons fresh lemon juice
- Sea salt, to taste
- Filtered water, as needed
- 1 tablespoon olive oil plus more for drizzling
- Pinch of cayenne pepper

How to Prepare:

1. In a blender, add all the ingredients and pulse until smooth.
2. Transfer the hummus into a large bowl and drizzle with oil.
3. Sprinkle with cayenne pepper and serve immediately.

Preparation time: 10 minutes

Total time: 10 minutes

Servings: 12

Nutritional Values:

- *Calories 129*
- *Total Fat 7.4 g*
- *Saturated Fat 0.9 g*
- *Cholesterol 0 mg*
- *Sodium 19521 mg*
- *Total Carbs 12.2 g*
- *Fiber 3.3 g*
- *Sugar 1.2 g*
- *Protein 4.7 g*

DESSERT RECIPES

Oat Cookies

Ingredients:

- 2 teaspoons chia seeds
- ¼ cup warm filtered water
- 2 cups quick oats, divided
- ½ teaspoon baking soda
- ½ teaspoon ground cinnamon
- ¼ teaspoon ground nutmeg
- ¼ teaspoon ground ginger
- ¼ cup raisins
- 1 large apple, peeled, cored, and chopped

- 4 Medjool dates, pitted and chopped
- 1 teaspoon apple cider vinegar
- 2 tablespoons cold water

How to Prepare:

1. Preheat your oven to 375 degrees F. Line a large cookie sheet with a large greased parchment paper.
2. In a bowl, mix together warm water and chia seeds.
3. Set aside until thickened.
4. In a large food processor, add 1 cup of the oats and pulse until finely ground.
5. Transfer the ground oats to a large mixing bowl.
6. Add the remaining oats, baking soda, spices, and raisins and mix well.
7. Now, in the blender, add the remaining ingredients and pulse until smooth.
8. Transfer the pureed mixture into the bowl with oat mixture and mix well.
9. Add the chia seeds mixture and stir to combine.
10. Spoon the mixture onto the prepared cookie sheet in a single layer and flatten each cookie slightly with your finger. Make sure the cookies are the same size to ensure they bake evenly.
11. Bake for about 12 minutes or until golden brown.

12. Remove from oven and place the cookie sheet on a wire rack to cool for about 5 minutes.
13. Now, invert the cookies onto the wire rack to cool before serving.

Preparation time: 15 minutes
Cooking time: 12 minutes
Total time: 27 minutes
Servings: 18

Nutritional Values:

- *Calories 68*
- *Total Fat 0.8 g*
- *Saturated Fat 0.1 g*
- *Cholesterol 0 mg*
- *Sodium 36 mg*
- *Total Carbs 14.5 g*
- *Fiber 2 g*
- *Sugar 6.6 g*
- *Protein 1.6 g*

Banana Cookies

Ingredients:

- 1 large banana, peeled and sliced
- ¾ cup unsweetened coconut, shredded
- ¼ teaspoon organic vanilla extract

How to Prepare:

1. Preheat your oven to 350 degrees F. Line a cookie sheet with a large piece of greased parchment paper.
2. In a large food processor, add all the ingredients and pulse until well combined.
3. Spoon the mixture onto the prepared cookie sheet and flatten each cookie slightly with your fingers. Make sure the cookies are the same size to ensure they bake evenly.

4. Bake for 25 minutes or until golden brown.

5. Remove from oven and place the cookie sheet on a wire rack to cool for about 5 minutes.

6. Carefully invert the cookies onto the wire rack to cool completely before serving.

Preparation time: 10 minutes

Cooking time: 25 minutes

Total time: 35 minutes

Servings: 4 <u>**these cookies are for 4 evenly divided servings**</u>

Nutritional Values:

- *Calories 84*
- *Total Fat 5.1 g*
- *Saturated Fat 4.5 g*
- *Cholesterol 0 mg*
- *Sodium 3 mg*
- *Total Carbs 10.1 g*
- *Fiber 2.2 g*
- *Sugar 5.1 g*
- *Protein 0.9 g*

Blueberry Muffins

Ingredients:

- ½ cup rolled oats
- ¼ cup almond flour
- 2 tablespoons flaxseeds
- ½ teaspoon baking soda
- ½ teaspoon ground cinnamon
- ¼ cup almond butter
- 1 organic egg
- 2 tablespoons mashed banana
- ¼ cup fresh blueberries

How to Prepare:

1. Preheat the oven to 375 degrees F. Lightly grease 10 cups of a muffin pan(s). **(This recipe uses a standard muffin tin that makes 10 muffins.)** Place all the

ingredients except the blueberries in a blender and pu.
until smooth and creamy.
2. Transfer the mixture into a bowl and fold in blueberries.
3. Transfer the mixture into the prepared muffin cups evenly.
4. Bake for about 10-12 minutes or until a toothpick inserted in the center comes out clean.
5. Remove from the oven and place the muffin tin on a wire rack to cool for about 10 minutes.
6. Carefully invert the muffins onto the wire rack to cool before serving.

Preparation time: 15 minutes
Cooking time: 12 minutes
Total time: 27 minutes
Servings: 10

Nutritional Values:
- *Calories 52*
- *Total Fat 2.7 g*
- *Saturated Fat 0.4 g*
- *Cholesterol 16 mg*
- *Sodium 71 mg*
- *Total Carbs 4.9 g*
- *Fiber 1.3 g*
- *Sugar 0.7 g*
- *Protein 2.1 g*

Ingredients:

- 4 large apples, cored and cut each into 8 equal sized slices

- 1/8 teaspoon ground cinnamon

- 2 tablespoons walnuts, chopped

How to Prepare:

1. Preheat the oven to 400 degrees F. Line a baking sheet with a piece of lightly greased parchment paper.

2. Arrange the apples onto the prepared baking sheet and roast for about 30-35 minutes.

116

3. Remove the sheet from the oven and transfer the apples to a platter.
4. Sprinkle with cinnamon and walnuts and serve.

Preparation time: 10 minutes
Cooking time: 35 minutes
Total time: 45 minutes
Servings: 6

Nutritional Values:

- *Calories 94*
- *Total Fat 18 g*
- *Saturated Fat 0.1 g*
- *Cholesterol 0 mg*
- *Sodium 1 mg*
- *Total Carbs 20.8 g*
- *Fiber 3.8 g*
- *Sugar 15.5 g*
- *Protein 1 g*

Spinach Sorbet

Ingredients:

- 3 cups fresh spinach, torn

- 1 tablespoon fresh basil leaves

- ½ an avocado, peeled, pitted, and chopped

- ¾ cup almond milk

- 20 drops liquid stevia

- 1 teaspoon almonds, chopped very finely

- 1 teaspoon organic vanilla extract

- 1 cup ice cubes

How to Prepare:

1. In a blender, add all the ingredients and pulse until creamy and smooth.
2. Transfer into an ice cream maker and process according to manufacturer's directions.
3. Transfer into an airtight container and freeze for at least 4-5 hours before serving.

Preparation time: 15 minutes
Total time: 15 minutes
Servings: 4

Nutritional Values:

- *Calories 166*
- *Total Fat 16 g*
- *Saturated Fat 10.6 g*
- *Cholesterol 0 mg*
- *Sodium 26 mg*
- *Total Carbs 5.7 g*
- *Fiber 3.2 g*
- *Sugar 1.9 g*
- *Protein 2.3 g*

Raspberry Ice Cream

Ingredients:

- 2¼ cups fresh raspberries, divided

- 1 small avocado, peeled, pitted, and chopped

- 10 dates, pitted and chopped

- ¼ cup cashews, soaked for 30 minutes and drained

- 1¾ cups unsweetened almond milk

- 2/3 cup filtered water

- 1 tablespoon fresh lemon juice

- 1 tablespoon fresh beet juice

How to Prepare:

1. In a blender, add 2 cups of raspberries and the remaining ingredients and pulse until creamy and smooth.
2. Transfer into an ice cream maker and process according to manufacturer's directions.
3. Transfer into an airtight container and freeze for at least 4-5 hours.
4. Top with the remaining raspberries and serve.

Preparation time: 15 minutes
Total time: 15 minutes
Servings: 6

Nutritional Values:

- *Calories 187*
- *Total Fat 11.5 g*
- *Saturated Fat 2.1 g*
- *Cholesterol 0 mg*
- *Sodium 102 mg*
- *Total Carbs 21.9 g*
- *Fiber 7.1 g*
- *Sugar 11.4 g*
- *Protein 3 g*

Mint Mousse

Ingredients:

- 1½ cups raw coconut meat, chopped
- 1 tablespoon fresh mint leaves
- 1 tablespoon chia seeds
- 1¼ cups unsweetened almond milk
- 12 drops liquid stevia
- ¼ cup almond butter
- 1 teaspoon organic vanilla extract
- 3 tablespoons fresh raspberries

How to Prepare:

1. In a blender, add all ingredients except the raspberries and pulse until creamy and smooth.
2. Transfer into serving bowls and refrigerate to chill before serving.
3. Garnish with raspberries and serve.

Preparation time: 15 minutes
Total time: 15 minutes
Servings: 4

Nutritional Values:

- *Calories 149*
- *Total Fat 12.9 g*
- *Saturated Fat 9 g*
- *Cholesterol 0 mg*
- *Sodium 63 mg*
- *Total Carbs 8.1 g*
- *Fiber 5.1 g*
- *Sugar 2.3 g*
- *Protein 2.4 g*

Chocolate Tofu Mousse

Ingredients:

- 1 pound firm tofu, drained
- ¼ cup unsweetened almond milk
- 2 tablespoons cacao powder
- 10-15 drops liquid stevia
- 1 tablespoon organic vanilla extract
- ¼ cup fresh strawberries

How to Prepare:

1. In a blender, add all ingredients except the strawberries and pulse until creamy and smooth.

2. Transfer into serving bowls and refrigerate to chill for at least 2 hours.

3. Garnish with strawberries and serve.

Preparation time: 15 minutes
Total time: 15 minutes
Servings: 6

Nutritional Values:

- *Calories 67*
- *Total Fat 3.7 g*
- *Saturated Fat 0.9 g*
- *Cholesterol 0 mg*
- *Sodium 17 mg*
- *Total Carbs 2.9 g*
- *Fiber 3.5 g*
- *Sugar 1 g*
- *Protein 6.6 g*

Bean Brownies

Ingredients:

- 2 cups cooked black beans
- 12 Medjool dates, pitted and chopped
- 2 tablespoons almond butter
- 2 tablespoons quick rolled oats
- 2 teaspoons organic vanilla extract
- ¼ cup cacao powder
- 1 tablespoon ground cinnamon

How to Prepare:

1. Preheat the oven to 350 degrees F. Line a large baking dish with parchment paper.

2. In a food processor, add all the ingredients except the cacao powder and cinnamon and pulse until well combined and smooth.
3. Transfer the mixture into a large bowl.
4. Add the cacao powder and cinnamon and stir to combine.
5. Now, transfer the mixture into the prepared baking dish evenly and smooth the surface of the mixture with the back of a spatula.
6. Bake for about 30 minutes.
7. Remove from oven and place on a wire rack to cool completely.
8. With a sharp knife, cut into 12 equal sized brownies and serve.

Preparation time: 15 minutes
Cooking time: 30 minutes
Total time: 45 minutes
Servings: 12

Nutritional Values:
- *Calories 216*
- *Total Fat 2.3 g*
- *Saturated Fat 0.5 g*
- *Cholesterol 0 mg*
- *Sodium 2 mg*
- *Total Carbs 43.3 g*
- *Fiber 8 g*
- *Sugar 18.9 g*
- *Protein 9 g*

Conclusion

The main agenda of the alkaline diet is to add veggies and fruits to your diet without any special ingredients or supplements. Although the diet is going to be hard for certain people and those of you who are frequent travelers but, it does offer loads of health benefits. With the alkaline diet, we recommend you start and maintain a proper exercise routine to boost your weight loss. You should exercise for a minimum of 150 minutes a week to get the most from the alkaline diet.